I0792336

Preparation Tools

Greater efficiency.

Graeme Smith

PUBLISHED ON AMAZON.COM
BY
LABYRINTH BOOKS

3

DEDICATION:

This book is dedicated to my family.
  Hele-ly (Ly).
        my wife:

  Ingrid.
        our daughter:

  Marie.
        my former wife:

  Fiona, Natalie and Michael
        our children:

  Georgie
        Michael's wife:

  Pearl, Kiki and Martha.
        their children:

They have put up with me for many years and I thank them for that.
I hope this book gives an insight into what occupied me much of the time.
All have done worthwhile and interesting things in the absence of my help.
I congratulate them for their achievements.

SUPPORT:
  Support International Artist magazine:
        contact: editor@internationalartist.com
  Support the Australian Artist magazine:
        contact: editor@australianartist.com

HOW TO USE THIS BOOK:

Usually people don't think through things to the level they need to.
Because of that, they have projects instead of tasks on their "to do" list.
That leads to procrastination for it hasn't been broken down to a task level.
So go through your book once to understand it THEN go through it again.

Then start at the PART of the book that interests you MOST.
Make notes of the steps you will need to take and the resources required.
Use notes to create a step by step system for implementing ideas.
Often you won't refer back to an original if you've created **YOUR** system.

The first question to ask and answer is "Why is this being done?"
How does this align with where you want to get to?
What are the strategic implications of doing this?
Does this fit in with getting to a goal in the shortest and fastest time?
What would it be like if it were totally successful?
Define it - what is success for this project and how will you know?

Now brainstorm all the tasks are involved in your project.
It's important not to go linear too fast with this.
By linear, I mean step one, step two, step three, and step four.
You end up cutting off options.
As you plan step one, two, three, there is a specific step that might be four.
Start steps too quickly, other ways for one, two and three may not appear.

The first third of a brainstorming session is easy - find lots of ideas.
The second third is challenging – look at the ideas to see where they go.
Then push to think outside the box for that's often where the big idea is!
That's where the most powerful way of getting a project done the fastest is.

Most never get to that level and end up short-changing themselves.

Then their project takes longer and they also set up to procrastinate.

This final brainstorming part of the equation is incredibly important.

Once you've brainstormed a project put options in a linear sequence.

Then you can figure out what you've overlooked and all becomes obvious.

Get tasks in order, add missing steps, and lay out your list for the project.

When you've organized the tasks into a linear process decide:

What things can you start immediately?

What can start that is not dependent on things that must occur beforehand?

There may be five, six or twenty that don't rely on anything else to happen.

You can get started on them right away!

Write things you think of and cross off things as you do them.

Add in stuff that is relevant from time to time.

INDEX:

INTRODUCTION:

Would you like to be a successful artist?
Preparation Tools help you get organized, essential for a successful artist.
Use them in conjunction with your present approaches.
Also in conjunction with other strategies in other programs.

Success seems mythical, which is why I've termed it the Holy Grail.
The Crusaders of old travelled the world seeking it.
For professional artists the Holy Grail is to create more sales and build income.

So how will you know you are a success?
That's for you to decide but consider these comments:

'Strong self-discipline and intelligent self-management are in my view the fundamental building blocks for all success.' (p77)
There will be disappointments along the way, that's how we learn. Each disappointment is a test of your commitment. They also add to your experience and strength. In the end your commitment is the key to your success.
(Don Talbot – Australian swimming coach in "Nothing but the best")

If you are to be successful then you need to be well organized!
Elite athletes reap rewards by investing in themselves.
So should artists.
BUT if you put it off it will never happen!

But there can be no half measures.
If you want to be a successful artist then you must do the job properly.
Either do it or forget it!

You can gain knowledge.

Until you acquire experience acting on that knowledge you won't move ahead.
You will stay at your present state!

This is won't happen straight away.
It won't even happen at all!
Unless you know why you need a professional approach to your career.
The way of the leisure artist will not get you there!

In a manner not previously possible you can set up your future earnings.
It will take time and a little money in the beginning.
But if you wait until Christmas, next year, whenever the 'right' time to start is,
All that happens is the whole process is delayed.
There needs to be much work done.

But with little actual expense initially, a start can be made if time is there.
You will build, or maybe re-build, the foundations of your artistic journey!

Possibly other things might need to be foregone, delayed or accelerated.
To facilitate a speedy transition to this new phase of your artistic career.

If you want to be a professional artist then painting well is not sufficient.
Many artists do that!
You also need to be successful as a business.
That's quite different!

Visualize success.
Success is getting to another level.
Imagine what that will actually feel like when you experience it.
Then you'll be more determined to make it a reality.
If you can think it, you can achieve it!

Praise people around you.
By helping others build their self-confidence, they might in turn boost yours.
Just as importantly you'll appreciate ways confidence can be built.

Develop a sense of self-belief.
Make decisions based on the belief that you can do what you set out to do.

Don't give failure a chance.
Become more competent.
Set goals to improve your ability, skills and knowledge.
Do this regularly and consistently.
Even champion sports people practice regularly!
Usually this is more than those who are not champions!

Believe in yourself.
This is the first step on the path to success.
So you must at least have done this to some degree.
Now build from that beginning and make a series of small additional steps.
Reflect back from time to time to appreciate progress that you have made.

Grow through experience.
You will grow every time you rise to a challenge and learn something.
Sometimes this is what not to do, at other times it will be worth repeating.
Savor successes.
At first they might be small, but that's how everyone starts.
Keep track of them for that helps you realize later successes are better.

Turn negative situations into positive ones.
View mistakes as problems or challenges.
They are at least opportunities to gain experience.
So increase your opportunities.
Expand your network of people.

Through new relationships, you open the way to new opportunities. With new opportunities comes increasing confidence.

Surround yourself with success.
Mix with people who are successful and you'll learn to behave as they do. You'll build your confidence and be inspired by their attitudes.

Remember too, success is a journey not a destination.
You do not attain success but become successful.

A: PRODUCTIVITY AIDS:

1. Diary
2. Yearly Planner
3. Ideas Book
4. Procedures Manual
5. Job Descriptions
6. Organization Chart
7. Career Audit

1. Diary

Do you have a diary?
It's not just for recording events past, as is traditional with a diary.
It should have dates and times of events that are planned and scheduled.

Carry it with you and it becomes indispensable (could be electronic).
Regularly update from your Yearly Planner and keep it near your phone.
Eventually everything you do from the start until the end of a day.
For at least the current week will be in your Diary.

Update each day before you leave where you work (studio).
Then you can mentally plan for the following day.
This is just another part of your systems for running your art effectively.

2. Yearly Planner

Do you have a yearly planner?
Enter dates of exhibitions, delivery, works sold, and other important date.
They can all be seen at a glance on the Yearly Planner.

Then it is easy to keep track of longer term events in your career.
Also how they might clash with your personal life too.
You can plan ahead for regular revisions to your Procedures Manual.

Buy a blank yearly planner from any office supplies store.
It may pay to create your own larger version for the studio wall instead.

The hard part is keeping a Yearly Planner up to date.
Check regularly to add new events and mark off those no longer relevant.
If you forget to do this your planner's usefulness diminishes!
So include regular revision times on your planner (say weekly).

Eventually all you do from the start of a year until the end is there.
You may even have next year's planner under way too.

This is one system you develop for running your art business.
As with the other ideas it takes some time to set up.
But then will save considerable wastage of your time.

If people want to know when something happens.
Refer them to the planner.

3. Ideas Book

You are probably familiar with a sketchbook.
Well here's a similar idea.
But for non-artistic aspects of your art journey.

It can be any book you like.
It doesn't really matter whether it has lines or the pages are blank.
Write, scribble, draw, make notes, or otherwise put down your ideas.
Then it ends up being full of your ideas, or memory aids for your ideas.

The ideas are about your artistic career and how you'll create it.
Writing down thoughts is a way to commit them to your memory bank.
Then they are accessible later.

Naturally paintings are there as aspects of your business.
Rather than as evidence of creativity.

Look at various pages in your Ideas Book at some later date.
That will refresh your ideas beyond what is merely recorded in your book.
But you are not limited to only using the book for that.

Can you translate the general into the particular?
Often when you read something it is expressed in a very general nature.
So can you translate the general ideas into something of use to you?
When that happens it's more likely that you'll do something as a result.

But unless you do something, no changes are made.
Everything is just an intellectual exercise.
By writing your ideas down you are starting to build a bridge.
It's between the general principles and actions you can take.

Do you plan effectively?
A business that fails to plan, plans to fail.
It's as true of artists as it is of any other kind of business.

Your Ideas Book is where you start planning.
Sometimes this will be repetitive, as minor variations are tested.
But they have to be worked through to find out what happens.

Effective planning is the beginnings of effective action.
Your plans are the test runs for the real world.
But plans by themselves don't make anything happen.
Although they certainly ease the way.

The better prepared the more likely it is you'll be successful.
Your preparation can even be quite systematic!

How will you get the most from your Ideas Book?
You always get more from what you write rather than read or hear.
If you do not try anything then there is no chance of an improvement at all.
So sensible ideas mean a chance to improve on what you did before.

Your success making changes depends on many factors.
Just what stage of your career are you at right now?
It's easier for a beginner to show great improvement.
Than if you have been around for a while.

What methods are you using right now?
Most importantly, how determined are you?
Are you adaptable?
Is your new approach systematic and sensible?

Here are some tips.

Take your time.
Make changes at a moderate pace, but do make them.
It's like the tortoise and the hare, slow and steady wins the race.

Things often start simply and get more complex as time goes by.
If the simple starting points (the basics) are neglected.
Understanding the later complexities is impossible.

Stick to the basics.
Whatever they are, once you decide, stick with them for a reasonable time.
Give them time to have an effect for the basic are not just the beginnings.
They're the fundamentals.
So they are an inherent part of every aspect of being a successful artist.

Theory and practice go together.
When you've decided on some action, do it.
Test the theory and find out whether it works or not.

Either way you have knowledge you didn't have before.
Remember the first time you do something it feels strange and awkward.
In time a new idea will feel more natural, which is why practice is needed.

We all have times in our career that are less than ideal,
No matter who you are, what you have or what you've accomplished.
What can you do to overcome those times?
How do you remind yourself of what's important and get back on track?
That's where your Ideas Book can help.

Here's an important question to consider on those occasions:
What ideas would help you be better in your professional career?
Those thoughts will need to be fully integrated into your way of thinking.
If you could see the world in a way that would make success more certain.
What would you need to believe?

Your Ideas Book can help you keep a realistic perspective.
There are peaks and valleys in a career.

Sometimes, they're unavoidable.

Both are temporary.
By having a record of the times you've struggled.
Remind yourself of what worked to overcome past negative situations.
But keeping an Ideas Book can do even more for you than that.

Is there a way to be more optimistic, happier, and think better?
What if it took you less than five minutes a day to do?
But you reaped the rewards all day long!

Would you want to know it?
And more importantly would you do it?
That's why I strongly recommend you start developing this habit.
Write out those things you're grateful for along with the reasons why
On a daily basis.

In less than a few weeks' notice the difference in your thinking.
Keep it up for a few months and notice the difference to your bottom line.

Have you started your Ideas Book yet?
What effect have you noticed?

4. Procedures Manual

Do you have a procedures manual?
Just about all franchises have procedures manuals.

That's also why franchises are a very effective business model.
Everyone knows what they are must to do so the business works.

So how should you go about creating one?
The first step is to develop a computer file outlining your career approach.
This covers action steps or procedures taken to do anything important.

Important things that just must be done right or a poor job results.
For example exactly how works are wrapped and delivered to clients.

It could be things done a certain way as that's how you do them.
They are a part of your brand or personality.
You are a western artist and so never seen in public without a Stetson.

They could also be things that are only done occasionally.
Writing down what has to be done means you do not forget next time.
That's a lot of work.

It needs to be broken down into manageable chunks.
Initially just create an outline of the main elements of your art career.
You might consider studio operations, marketing, finance, and so on.
Develop a list of procedures (action steps) to accompany the headings.
At this stage you just list those procedures.

The next step:
Now when you encounter a problem, write it down.
Document the procedures (or steps) to be taken to solve that problem.

Put that onto your loose-leaf procedures manual or computer file.
If the problem reappears at a later date, go to the procedure and follow it.

If changes are needed make them and add the new procedure.
Then over time important procedures get developed into even better ones.

Do you happen to employ anyone (an agent)?
Then they can contribute in a similar manner to your manual.

Deal with three or four procedures a month (even if no problems).
Eventually all you do from the start of a day until the end is there.
What you are now developing are systems for running your art career.

Anybody can use it!
It might even be the basis for franchising or selling to other artists!

It also saves considerable wastage of your time (but not to start with).
If people want to know how something is done, refer them to the manual.
Document just one procedure a week so that is 50 or so in a year!
If they are the most urgent a large chunk of frustrating situations are gone.

But regularly review aspects that give problems.
Some things will come naturally, whilst others take some time to assimilate.
The tough areas leave alone for a while.
But do return to them at regular intervals.
If you persist sufficiently the breakthrough will come.
There are no 'golden bullets' to success - it's a battle all the way.

There are always topical items to consider.
But it is also important that other issues are considered on a regular basis.
Otherwise they can become completely overlooked.

A 'Standard Agenda' eliminates this problem.
They are a code for items that should be discussed at some time.

Minute Code 17/10/22   Date Entered 05/11/22   Review Date 05/23
At the end of a meeting 4 or 5 are selected for discussion next time.
Along with any business carried over from the present meeting.

Procedures must be understood and standardised.
Procedures are written in a language people using them are familiar with.
Such as photographs, diagrams, maps, charts, or computer files.
Use other way to record if they are appropriate for some or all aspects.

There could be different procedure for different aspects of a career.
These differences could relate to different types of meetings being held.
Care will need to be taken to ensure any overlaps are consistent.
Some procedures will be reviewed weekly (at first) others monthly.
And even at less frequent but regular intervals (three monthly).

All procedures should be reviewed annually at least.
Review Dates and next occurrence are entered on the Yearly Planner.
If appropriate add to relevant Portfolio Outline.

Developing a procedure.
Form a written proposal with what is not liked about the present situation.
Include budgeting details if relevant.
Provide any relevant people with a copy of the proposition.

Allocate specific meeting time for input and comment.
Proposition adjusted if necessary.
Re-present for further comment and consensus if necessary.
Decide course of action and schedule implementation of action.
Take necessary action and if necessary take additional action.

Evaluate results / outcomes of action.
Add to Members' Guide
Place review date or next occurrence on Yearly Planner.
If appropriate add to one or more Portfolio Outline.

But, you don't have to do it on your own either!
Build a support infrastructure leaving you time to focus on what you do best.
You have a team (gallery, picture framer, accountant, spouse, at least).

How can they become a champion team, instead of people who help?
People are naturally motivated if they can design their way to do things.
And also they put that into action.

That's why people go into business for themselves.
They work longer hours than when employed, or their own employees do.
Like you probably do if you are to be successful!

If people have the chance to design particular aspects of their work.
They're also similarly motivated.
This is because they're doing something for which they see a purpose.
Their job now has a rationale and can become more of a personal mission.

You'll often see this happen with work projects.
They seem to take on a life of their own!
People become highly motivated and usually enjoy what they're doing.

There's value in the outcome.
So people will often do things they wouldn't otherwise do because of that.
They are aware it's a means to a desirable end.
But they also enjoy most of the process anyway.

You can build conditions so your team is motivated the same way.
Your career becomes their project.
Then their natural motivation is harnessed and brings satisfaction to all.
Now that sounds like a pretty good thing doesn't it?

I recommend creating three procedure manuals.

To ensure your art career reaps full reward of the systems you develop,

Here they are:
The Role-Specific Manual.
The Functional Manual.
The Comprehensive Manual

Let's look at each of these separately.
Then you'll be clear how best to organize your business systems.
Which will help ensure that they'll be followed exactly as they're set out.

Role-Specific Procedures Manual.
The role-specific procedure manual documents tasks and activities.
That a person in a specific role is responsible for.
Procedures a person in a particular role does without involving others.

In this situation, the individual in a specific role is 100% in control.
So they are held 100% accountable.

Most manuals have 20 to 30 systems a person is responsible for.
There could be more or fewer though.
It really depends on the role.
Having role-specific manuals gives your people a sense of security.
They know exactly what's required of them.
They also know exactly how they must go about performing their tasks.

It also makes it incredibly easy to train the next person for the role.
A role-specific Manual is a training manual for future people filling the role.
Role-specific manuals are like doing an audit of all positions in a business.
They uncover any and all inefficiencies that might exist.
It will also reveal any roles that are currently under-leveraged.

Functional Procedures Manuals:

A functional procedure manual covers a series of processes or systems. They require close co-ordination of several team members for an outcome.'

The Comprehensive Manual.
A comprehensive manual has all systems and procedures for your career.
When most business owners think about a "procedure manual."
They are really thinking about a comprehensive manual.

It's a mistake to give everyone a copy of your comprehensive manual.
They don't need all the information inside it.
In addition it's usually too big to easily manage.
Plus, it puts your entire business in jeopardy.
Every employee has a complete view of everything done in your business.

A comprehensive procedure manual for you and a management team.
Every other team member will have a copy of other manuals:
Role-specific manuals and whatever functional manuals they participate in.

Developing your own Procedures Manuals.
You don't really go about creating a comprehensive manual.
Instead you create the role-specific and functional manuals.
By doing so you'll be building your comprehensive manual.

If you've got a team already.
Then assign each member to develop his or her own role-specific manual.
Managers should create their own role-specific manuals too.
But they should also create your functional manuals.

Whether or not you have a team create your own role-specific manual.

It'll give you the opportunity to improve your own performance.

And lay a foundation to ultimately hand responsibilities to a growing team.

Conclusion

Confidence, the key to success.

Don Talbot (elsewhere) mentions commitment is the key to success.

He is right, but confidence is the key to everything, including commitment.

Confidence determines the quality of your art.

Also the success of a career, the kind of relationships you have, everything.

Usually it seems as if you either have confidence or you do not.

Although you can have it in some areas but not in others.

Without confidence it's unreasonable to expect clients to believe in you.

Then they will not provide you with support you need so what do you do?

5. Job Descriptions

How does someone know what to do?
Avoid thinking that being a successful artist is only about painting well.
Make sure people you employ know what is expected of them.
Avoid problems with your agent by making sure all is clear from the start.
A job description is the agenda for a future Performance Appraisal meeting.

A job description overview.

JOB DESCRIPTION
Position (Agent)

POSITION
Position (Agent)

REPORTS TO
Artist

DUTIES
Common Tasks for all Employees

List tasks specific to the position of Agent

TOP PRIORITY KPIs
Important areas and measurable -
Reasons why you would keep the person in the position.

Ways to measure
Checklists &/or reporting mechanisms.

TEAM CONTRIBUTION & ACCOUNTABILITY
Key actions/updates/tasks to assist specific team members.
The team depends on these tasks being completed.

PERSONAL ATTRIBUTES:
Be responsible.
Ability to work unsupervised.
Conscientious.
Commitment to learn new tasks.
Good work ethic.
Open to suggestions.
Shows initiative.
Honesty.

SKILLS - required for position, what level?
Minimum education level.
Good communications.
Appropriate level of trade/technical skills.
Negotiation.
Experience (years).
Customer service.
Product knowledge.
Computing skill.
Software knowledge.

FUTURE DEVELOPMENT – for next six months.
External.
School, TAAFE.

Internal training.
Conferences.

SHORT to MEDIUM TERM OBJECTIVES.
Projects to accomplish rather than ongoing tasks.

REGULAR PERFORMANCE MANAGEMENT REVIEW & APPRAISAL.
Define when, by whom, how often, Preparation Tools, etc.

My Position.
Actively participate in weekly/monthly reviews/meetings.
Use (key documents/reports) and/or reports of all completed jobs.
Include individual or job team by (workshop) manager(s).
Receive semi-annual performance appraisal by artist/agent using Job Description.

My staff.
Conduct weekly/monthly reviews/meetings.
Use key documents/reports and/or reports of KPI's and goal achievement.
Done by the individual, you or the team.
Conduct semi-annual performance appraisal, using job descriptions and appraisal agenda.

____

Employee Signature   Date

____

Artist Signature   Date

6. An organization chart.

It's a plan of how an organization is set up.
You can use one even if you do not have any employees.

You don't have to do it on your own either!
Build a support infrastructure that leaves time to focus on what you do best.
You have a team available (gallery, picture framer, accountant, spouse,).
So how can they become a champion team, instead of people who help?

People are motivated if they design their own way of doing things.
And also to put that into action.

That's why people go into business for themselves.
They also work longer hours than they ever did as an employee.
Or indeed any of their own employees would.
Like you probably do if you are to be successful!

If people have the chance to design particular aspects of their work.
They're also similarly motivated.
This is because they're doing something for which they see a purpose.
Their job now has a rationale and can become more of a personal mission.

You'll often see this happen with work projects.
They seem to take on a life of their own!
People become highly motivated and usually enjoy what they're doing.
There's value in the outcome.
So people will often do things they wouldn't otherwise do because of that.
They are aware it's a means to a desirable end.
But they also enjoy most of the process anyway.

You can build conditions so your team is motivated in the same way.
Your career becomes their project.

When this happens, their natural motivation is harnessed.
That brings satisfaction to all.

7. A career audit.

A Career Audit forces us to put our brushes down and pick up a pen.
It invites one to step back and look at the bigger picture.
It leads to the realization.
You must become actively engaged in professional marketing.

Look at short and long term goals.
Ask yourself if your current behaviour is helping you achieve those goals.
And generally assess if you are headed in the right direction.

An Audit raises questions you may not think of asking yourself.
Or have been avoiding.

I like the format and the "sectional" delivery of the parts.
You have to think and respond in order to be rewarded with more.
It's effective." (Lesley White Prince George, Canada)

I found it gave me an Idea as to where I am now.
Interesting answering questions and brought a positive aspect to my life.
It gave me an idea what to do to improve and showed my weak points."

This was a real test.
It really made me think and use the dictionary too.
It was a major crisis for me because when I answered the questions.
I saw my answers were way off.

So it has made me
REALLY THINK ABOUT MY FUTURE AS AN ARTIST."
The way it is presented one step at a time is great.
You are excitedly waiting for the next step. (Kathy Kay – Mudgee, Australia)

"I finished Career Audit and see the chance of cutting my own keys.
The generic questions and answers put the onus on me to think for myself.
As opposed to another business-person taking care of all my problems.
The audit prompted my business thought processes."

Many artists think that they should only focus on the creative process.
They shy away from the business end.
Some "prince charming" dealer is going to take care of everything for them.
If an artist isn't serious about the business end, why should anyone else?
(Mireille Samson, Vancouver, Canada)

I think it is an invaluable method for artists
It forces the issue of professionalism to be considered in more detail.
I think it helps separate fact from fiction in the artist's mind.
It basically suggests a more realistic way of looking at things.
As well as sorting out whether this is a professional or hobby venture."
(Jo Simon, Auckland, New Zealand)

It made me look at my art career from a totally different perspective.
Your future directions really provoked a lot of thought.
I didn't get the answers right but possible solutions made sense of it all.
I can now see the direction I need to take.
Thank you once again.
(Bill Truslove, Victor Harbour, Australia)

Thanks for getting the wheels of my mind turning.
(Cindy Revell, Sherwood Park, Canada)

What is the Career Audit anyway?
THINK ABOUT YOUR CAREER in a more business like way than usual.
Put thoughts into practice and your future is less dream and more reality.
None of the Career Audit is about your creative work (how you paint etc.).

It's about everything else.

WHY should you do one?
We all need to stop and assess what we are doing from time to time.
The elements in the Career Audit get you to think about where you are at.
With your career right now.
That can help just about anyone who does it.

Your answers to the Career Audit are personal.
That applies even to quite OBJECTIVE questions.
A certain degree of vagueness allows a wide variety of answers.
It's a process that can be used by ANY artist, for each answers differently.

HOW OFTEN should you complete a Career Audit?
Every six months will allow a running check on your career progress.
You'll also be able reaffirm (or otherwise) where you are heading.

The FIRST audit tool is Present Challenges.
Present Challenges is for thinking where you are right now with your career.

It begins a process of SELF-ANALYSIS that many artists do not usually do.

Present Challenges, and the whole Career Audit, raises questions.

They are ones you may not think of asking yourself or have been avoiding.

B: YOUR CAREER:

1. Will you become a professional artist?
2. Just when do you start a career?
3. Framing is dressing up the work.
4. Success is an upward spiral.
5. Conclusion

1. Will you become a professional artist?

Distinguishing a hobby artist from a professional.
Was brought to my attention as a result of correspondence with artists.
They think an artist's only task is to paint (or whatever their art might be).
Life would indeed be simple if that was the case.

However, life is not that simple, even though it may appear so.
We think of things in isolation as when we seek to understand their nature.
But to apply those thoughts, they are related to many other concepts.
This makes simple propositions a complex amalgam of action possibilities.

One artist wanted me to stop referring to people as hobby artists.
She was not yet a full time practitioner but was serious and passionate.
She felt "hobby artist" when applied to people such as her was derogatory.
I think many artists share her belief.
A hobby artist is not serious about their painting just doing it as a past-time.
I guess most people would agree that such people are indeed hobby artists.

What distinguishes a hobby?
But let's look at other areas where people pursue a hobby for clarification.

Stamp-collectors, ball-room dancers, gardeners, cyclists pursue a hobby.
It is the passion that is the difference?

For a hobbyist in any field that is a distinguishing characteristic.
They spend a great deal of their waking hours on their hobby.
Those involved in a past-time do not have the passion of a hobbyist.
Sometimes due to time spent they branch into a related business.
Sell supplies, finished articles and lessons.
They also spend more time pursuing the hobby.

However, this doesn't always work out as expected!
Often the business is an impediment to continued enjoyment of the hobby.

This even applies to artists who follow their dream and paint full-time.
There is business which takes time from a studio but it has to be done.
Unless there's an independent income (spouse, retirement funds, wealth).
Maintaining the passion is now harder rather than easier.

Even worse the professional artist has to produce more works.
Because each work is a source of income.
So they can't take the same amount of time to complete each one.
Those with independent incomes are spared this pressure.

The best are sold but there is an increased stock of unsold works.
This is depressing and the passion can easily flicker at this point.
I thought of these things when I received the email referred to above.

So let's clarify the terms hobby artist, artist and professional artist.
Anyone who paints is an artist (they do art).

Professional artists earn income as a result of being an artist.
Just like professional tennis players or footballers or even card players.
Any artist who doesn't earn money Is a hobby artist.

They paint for the enjoyment and the satisfaction that it is possible.

To be a hobby artist is NOT a put-down but an accurate description.
An artist (hobby/professional) can be great or awful, most are in between.

Any artist (hobby / professional) may have a compulsion to paint.
But this is more common with a hobby artist, for it's their justification.
A professional must be dispassionate or they'll never sell anything.
Nor would there be sufficient works to develop and maintain an income.

So it's the passion that distinguishes the different artists.
Those who paint and enjoy it as an occasional activity are leisure artists.
Those passionate and do it as much as possible are bobby artists.
Those who earn an income are dispassionate as they create a business.

This doesn't mean the professional lacks dedication to their art.
They need that to sustain a career over hopefully many years.
Their dedication to their art allows them to continue painting.

There is nothing whatsoever wrong with being a hobby artist.
It's a perfectly worthwhile hobby.

Being an artist and being a professional artist are two different things.
Being an artist doesn't mean you understand how to be in business.
Being an artist is not necessary for running a successful art business.
If this were not so then how could galleries and agents survive?

A professional makes the business work in addition to being an artist.
There are many aspects which artists don't need to know anything about.
But a professional artist, gallery owner, or agent does.
Any art business must operate according to what it needs to flourish.

But you must have passion!

It's not an option for an artist when creating work.
That's why many artists write about their passion for their art.
There is nothing they want to do more than be at an easel and start painting.
Maybe you share this emotional attachment with your art too?

How do you find the right people and the right places?
How do you get attention at the right time to create demand for your work?

Decide where your work fits into the many niches of the art market.
Explore venues consistent with your career stage, talents and resources.
If you produce only originals research the fine art market.
This includes galleries, museums and known juried shows.

Mechanically reproduced multiples and crafts are at other venues.
They include the internet and through the wider retail market.

List individuals, organizations, public bodies who might show you.
Why might they invest time or money in your stuff over another artist?
This means looking from **their** point of view.

Methodically investigate any possible individual or group on your list.
Use the web, trade magazines, talk to or research artists who are there.
Assess what you gather against your criteria and art business goals.
Produce a short list that merits further in-depth investigation.
Systematically investigate each possible candidate on your short list.
Make e-mail inquiries, telephone calls and reconnaissance visits.
Find out if there might be a fit for your work.

There's a possibility that you work from home.
Your studio is the spare bedroom, or a garage, or is in the backyard.
These are the facts of life for many artists.

The economics may validate such an approach.

But it's not necessarily easier than the alternative of a studio elsewhere.

Home working needs discipline to separate business from personal.

This is particularly difficult for women.

They are usually under considerable expectations from family members.

Here are some steps for balancing your home and work.

But you must separate business from home.

If possible a separate studio and office to handle business related activities.

Not just painting but also phone calls etc.

Your supplies should be stored here too.

This separation will contribute to a more peaceful home environment.

It avoids reminders of your business with potential family resentment.

Your family is probably the major reason why you work from home anyway.

So you want things to be as harmonious as possible.

Also break large tasks into smaller ones.

It's said that you can eat an elephant if you take it one bite at a time.

This is true of anything.

A task that seems overwhelming needs to be broken into small parts.

They are then tackled, one at a time.

Have a deadline for completing each step if necessary.

This will develop time management skills.

You'll also learn what you can complete in a day at the same time.

Group errands.

Instead of something just when needed, do several things at the same time.

Having a list will help your planning.

So will when you grocery shop, return a library book and dry cleaning.
A box in the boot of a car for library books, mail and dry cleaning.
Then those tasks can be grouped with others of a more urgent nature.

Daily you'll receive unwanted mail and other material.
Unless it's something you actually need, throw it.
You could also have a donation box for clothes that have been outgrown.
Once it is full donate the no longer needed garments to a favourite charity.
Recycling is another de-cluttering activity.
Make this a habit and you'll never have that old stuff just lying around!

Get up at least 30 minutes earlier.
Then you can have some time for yourself before the day really begins.
Think of it as getting ahead time before you might otherwise fall behind.
Getting up early allows you to focus without interruptions.

Limit multi-tasking.
Tough for female readers, but the more you multi-task the less you focus.
Productivity is lower by 20% to 40% (depend on complexity) if multi-tasking.
Your brain works best when it focuses on a single activity.
That's your painting when you are at work.
Focus on your business or your family but not both at the same time.

Delegate.
Share those household tasks, even the younger children can do something.
As the family gets older they learn habits such as they will need as adults.

Plan your meals.
Take time to write your menu ideas for the coming week (each Sunday).
Then grocery shop to your plan.
In the evening, or first thing in the morning, check your menu plan.

Lay out any frozen items that might need to defrost.
Also pack your lunch when you prepare school meals for children.

For effective and enjoyable career get the home/work balance right.
Good planning will make this possible.

Do you want to be an employee or have a career?
If you can find someone to employ you as an artist, then that is a valid view.
On the other hand if you are in business as (say) Joe Bloggs artist.
Then someone has to do the business things!
A hobby view of art does not need to consider running a business.
Whereas a professional artist must.
It's your choice, so don't complain if business is tougher than it need be.
Because there was insufficient application given to that area.

What is required of the professional?
They must balance all aspects, business, practical, research, reading.
Everyone has to balance business, family, leisure and anything important.
None of this is simple or easy, but it should be done.

What can you do?
There are only 24 hours in a day and that applies to everyone.
But different people make better use of their time allocation than others.
Simply by better planning.
This is a practical way to deal with problems of inertia many artists have.

Theory is simple (usually).
Turning it into practice is the hard part and often complex.
But the hardest part of doing anything is the beginning.
Do you say 'too hard' hoping things improve, but do nothing, or have a go?
A professional artist takes time to run a business by reducing painting time.

They'll do this not because they want to, but because they know they must.

It's never too early to start thinking about your tax position.
If you have a hobby rather than a professional career.
Then you'll not be able to declare any income from that hobby.
But you won't be able to claim any expenses either.
That's because they are not part of helping you earn taxable income.
That seems fair enough.

What if you are unsure whether you have a hobby or a business?
Then you should consult the taxation office or an accountant.
Possibly before doing that, decide which you'd rather have.
If you want to be a hobby artist (in the taxation office sense).
Then make sure about levels of income you can earn, in your situation.
Before you declare that income to the taxation office and claim expenses.

You may need to limit sales so you don't go over an income threshold.
Then join business people unintentionally.
On the other hand, if you want to be a business.

You'll still need to know the minimum you need to earn.
Before the TAXATION OFFICE will let you be registered as such.
To qualify there might be a special sales effort at the end of a financial year.

It's a good idea to maintain records of income and expenses.
Even if you are a hobby artist.
Then, will you be able to keep track of the financial cost of your hobby.
You'll also be able to take best advantage of any move to business ranks.

So what sort of records should you keep?
Well any receipt that has to do with earning money from your art.
Whether or not it is income in the TAXATION OFFICE sense.

You'd be surprised what you can justify as income earning expenses.
Naturally there are things like paints, paper, canvas, easels and so on.
But electricity for the studio, telephone, fax, mobile phone, and other items.

Don't forget about business trips either.
They are calling on galleries, visit exhibition, attend art society sessions.
Also visit other artists (advice, help), painting trips, gather information.
Accommodation, petrol, food and other sundries would all be part of this.

Then there's your car or van.
You must keep records of its business use for the TAXATION OFFICE.
It's worth doing, because even the little trips (to buy some turps) all add up.

What about your studio?
Such things as rates and interest repayments on loans for its construction.
Telephone, heating and cooling, repairs, additions and what you think of.

A studio is part of your house, as is likely, then the situation is trickier.
If you have a room or garage, then its size relative to the whole house.
In my case it is one third, but yours could be one tenth, or whatever.
Then claim this proportion of total rates, etc. applying to the whole house.
That's if you are a business and not a hobby,

All of these expenses actually cost money.
So there's no reason to go spending freely on things you don't really need.
Just because you can justify it as a business expense.
Unless you have surplus money.

On the other hand, for business spending that you really need to do.
There's no reason why it should cost tax as well (apart from GST).

Decide whether you want your art to be a business or hobby.
Do you believe you can be professional?
There's no way your dreams will come true unless you believe they can.
Even lottery winners have to believe, or they wouldn't buy tickets.

So is success one of your dreams?
Dreams are the foundation for beliefs.
The key to happiness is having dreams.
The key to success is making your dreams come true.

So can you make your dreams come true?
We're all working at making our dreams come true.

How can we turn this into reality and become successful?
Full time artists, making their dream come true, show it's possible.
There are also many who would like to be.
These people have a dream and they want to make it come true.
Fulltime artists provide the inspiration for those dreams becoming a reality.
They keep the dream alive.

Having your work in a gallery might be an important part of the dream.
Understanding how to go about it will certainly make the journey easier.
But it's not easy, for you actually have to do it.

So, if you want to approach some galleries.
In other words, have your work sold in a gallery.
The first step is to get started.
Just do it!

A professional artist is one who sells artworks.
This might be a full-time career but it can be done while in another career.
It all depends on the amounts of money earned AND time spent.
The amount of time taken to earn that money is also a key factor.

Each time you do something artistic you create a work.
They might be of varying standards too.
As time passes the number of such works usually rises.
Your artistic activity eventually creates pressure to a professional career.

So plan now for the future you desire.
This is quite easy, even if you do not yet know what your future holds.

For example do NOT frame anything!
No frame = save money.

Another thing is just have four or five sizes for any artwork you do.
This will mean more money saved on future framing.
That's because a small number of sizes means a limited frame range.
Then they can be swapped around.

Some people say all art is a niche market.
In the overall scheme of things, they're probably right.
So you need to position yourself as an artist!

Positioning is about how you present yourself.
Do this in such a way that you are clearly identified by your target market.
This is particularly important if you are aiming to fill a niche market.

Decide what you really want to do as an artist.
Which means you can position yourself so others think of you this way too.

Only take commissions in the area you seek to be known for.
Paint portraits if that's your thing, but not cats and dogs.
Do local paintings but not abstracts, nor portraits.
It's up to you what you want to be known for, but don't dilute the message.

Let's say you specialize in painting cats and dogs (raining down).
Then you must be positioned as **THE** artist for pet owners.
But, it's not just any pet is it?
It's really the cat and dog owners who need to know you're **THEIR** artist.

You'll need to love cats and dogs for a start.
You probably will have (at least) a pet dog and/or cat.
It's quite likely you'll attend cat and/or dog shows.
The local pet shops should know you and your art.
They can provide an important link to your intended clients.

You could even specialize in particular breeds.
This could be classic pet breeds.
Particularly those loved by the show winners, breeders or other groups.
They are also likely to pay most for paintings of their animals too.

You seek people who will pay quite a deal of money for a pet portrait.
Although it's quite possible these people don't attend pet shows at all.
They buy from breeders and live in luxury apartments or houses.
Breeders, who attend pet shows, are a key to unlock your market.

The breeders need to know some of benefits you offer their clients:
They'll own the painting for a lifetime, even after the pet passes away.
Thus the painting provides great memories for the pet owner.
Your painting will also be a great conversation piece.
It's a very personal gift for a pet lover too.

2. When does an art career start?

Most people start art by learning how to paint, draw, etc.
During this period they produce studies, sketches and other products.
At some point they apply what they learn and produce artworks.
Those artworks accumulate.
With this accumulation comes pressure about what to do with them.

They have four choices.
Let them pile up, destroy them, give them away or sell them.
Another choice is to combine these possibilities.
Many choose to sell and so become professional artists.

But usually they do not think of themselves as professional artists.
But they are, although without the knowledge required to be successful.

Are you contemplating a professional career rather than pursuing it?
Then you are likely to have a number of questions you'd like answered.
Let's look at a few of them.

You do not need to paint in any particular style.
You need confidence in whatever style you use which should be your
own.
The history of art is evidence that almost anything goes.
What and how you paint influences options but not can you have one.

Can you promote your beliefs?
Focus on beliefs in choosing what you do and you are painting
propaganda.
Even though you believe (even passionately) in the cause.
You will limit your chances of success to a client who share your views.
You are very unlikely to sell to those who do not.

Basically this is a form of advertising aimed at changing people.
It is usually used in this manner.

It is optimistic to expect sales success unless the theme is already popular.

Should you accept advice?
Perhaps you fear there will be a loss of your identity?
But why limit yourself just because the advice is available to other people?
Maybe you are worried that all who accept advice will do the same thing?
It depends what the advice is about.

If it is similar to how you should paint a house (or whatever).
Then your fears may be well founded.

On the other hand it could be here is a way to attract more clients.
Can it matter if other artists are using the same way if their work is different?

What if you only have one day a week for painting?
If you only have a full day a week for a professional career.
Whether painting or doing other professional stuff or both.

It is doubtful whether you can be a professional artist.
A career requires more time than that.

That means your first MAJOR task is to address the time problem.
It is a hard decision for you can't be a professional artist on a day a week.
At best you could be a part-time professional artist.
Even this will require addressing the time issues already touched on.

Just painting will never let you be a professional artist!
So the first priority is to make your career a habit.
So no matter how short a time allocation, make it regular and systematic.

Everyone is subject to the limitations of time, including artists.
Time must be found to do the works AND also run a career (however done).
As well as for family, leisure and other less predictable happenings.
Prioritising is a key technique for dealing with this.

So time management is a major skill in achieving anything.

Putting thoughts into practice is not necessarily easy at all.
Even with painting, an artist needs to consider relationships.
Such as between tones, colours, subject matter, technique and so on.
In order to arrive at a desired result.

An artist, who believes their only task is to paint, has prioritized.
But they haven't thought through the nature of being an artist.
It's like a butcher saying, my job is to cut meat.
But another says I'm running a butcher shop as well as cutting the meat.
The first butcher is an employee, but the second is in business.

Then we also need to take into account another time problem.
Actions can only be done in a time sequence.
It's just not possible to do everything all at the same time.

A lady was 22 years old and had her own business for the first time.
It didn't take her long to go out of business.
But not due to a lack of sales.

It was because she was uneducated on keeping records.
She could have been an artist couldn't she?
A top reason small businesses fail is their financial house is not in order.

So get some advice.
If you've never been in business for yourself.
Or if you struggle with managing your finances.
Good advice is an investment that could prove crucial to your survival.
It may be as simple as meeting with an accountant to get advice.
Find a business owner for advice on running a profitable business.

Create a budget.
When starting a career, your income will fluctuate.

It is important to have a budget for business and personal expenses.

Base the budget on lowest or average income, rather than highest income.

Your budget has tax payments, marketing, education, Internet, phone.

Manage your expenses.

Avoid carrying debt but some may be necessary, especially at the start.

Invest in marketing to show you are open and looking for clients.

If you need to borrow, don't take on more than you can easily pay off.

Manage debts by paying on time so you avoid additional charges.

Use lowest interest rate credit cards or loans, pay as soon as possible.

Only incur debts that are absolutely necessary.

Financial tools make it easier, more accurate, less time consuming.

Billing, expenses, taxes and other financial tasks are overwhelming.

Even those in business for a while find managing their finances intimidating.

Getting and keeping a financial house in order makes things less stressful.

Do not overspend, have enough money for savings, investment, retirement.

Track expenses, income, invoices and past due invoices, estimated taxes.

Not keeping track can cause your business to fail or give legal problems.

Put money aside every time you make a deposit.

Set a percentage of income aside for savings and charitable donations.

There are multiple reasons for doing this.

The main one is you have money "for a rainy day" and also a saving habit.

But more important are the psychological benefits you get from this habit.

Track whether you are "on schedule.

Track day by day if you are on schedule to hit income and wealth targets.

Those targets should be for the week, month, quarter and year.

Assessing where you are frequently, you can correct when you fall behind.

Otherwise it may be too late to correct your course to reach financial goals.

There is no retirement funded by someone else when you are an artist.

That means you are entirely responsible for your own retirement.

But setting up a retirement plan can help shelter your business profit.

I am not a financial advisor, so I'd advise you to seek professional counsel.

The main point is to set up a retirement plan and start saving immediately.

Let's be somewhat blunt, do you have what it takes?

Perhaps you may find what I'm about to say offensive but it has to be said.

No, there's no bad language, violence, or graphic sexual content.

But what I write may be disturbing to some readers.

I'm asking you to answer these questions:

Do you really have what it takes to earn a full-time income?

As a successful, moneymaking professional artist.

So you can comfortably, even extravagantly, support you and your family?

Are you kidding and wasting time and limited spare cash on a pipe dream?

That you don't actually have the courage and passion to make happen?

Are you ready to join those who have got what it takes to persevere?

And create a lucrative business as a professional artist?

Maybe you are a magic bullet seeker wanting a get rich or famous pill?

Are you in the first action-taker category with potential to succeed?

If you fall into the second category of dreamers.

Don't be offended, but consider not continuing to waste your time.

Some time ago I read a study that said:
21% of Americans see winning a lottery as a key wealth building strategy.
Another 14.9% are relying on an inheritance to carry them through.
Now the odds of winning a major jackpot are said to be 1 in 175 million.
Of the 20% of Americans who will inherit, most receive less than $49,000.
That's can buy a nice new car, but not enough to fund a carefree retirement.

Millions rely on gambling and death to secure a financial future.
I doubt if there would be much difference anywhere else in the world either.

If I lower the price of what I sell (like this book).
AND gloss over the reality of starting a new artistic career.
AND it was irresistible to people looking for a magic artistic bullet.
I'd make a lot of money!

But that's not what I'm about!
Starting any business takes … work!
Continuing that same business still takes … work!

Also it's not me that will build your art business for you.
Although I'm quite prepared to help you apply business building strategies.
So you can create your own professional career.

BUT you need to take responsibility for yourself, and do the work.
If you're not interested, it already sounds too hard, then stop reading now.
Go and buy a lottery ticket, or have a cup of coffee.
Spend the rest of your day watching television, or even painting.

Do you focus on the end result of success stories?
Rather than the process of getting there.

And make blind, almost frantic attempts to duplicate them.
Rather than strategically applying the lessons hidden within.
To create unique, lasting success which is all your own.

It may take 3 to 5 years for you to hit the jackpot, but so what?
An action-taker is inspired by what's possible with perseverance.
A six-figure income in 3 to 5 years as a professional artist is a great goal.
It's also a reasonable goal if you're prepared to train, learn, and focus.
But too many people aren't prepared to do the work!

A problem is unless your art business already has a solid foundation.
A proven ability to convert maximum traffic into long-term repeat clients.

You'll be trying to run before you've even learned to walk!
Advanced strategies which exponentially grow your wealth will **NOT** work.
Until you've laid a solid foundation for your business.

So what are the basics?
Defining your USP (unique selling proposition)
Strategically position yourself among your competition
Designing your website to sell
Writing compelling sales copy
Accepting credit card payments
Capturing opt-in email addresses
Creating a backend sales process
If you haven't done these things FIRST, all other efforts are wasted.

Look at artists who enjoy long-term success.
You'll quickly discover they're all founded on the basic principles outlined.
You can't expect to vacation like a rock star!
Stories of multi-million dollar vacations, rich hobbies, endless free time.
If you want it today is not a realistic expectation.

Can you make hundreds of thousands $$$ as a professional artist?
Absolutely!
Can you make millions?
It's possible, yes.
But this is NOT how millionaire of any kind got their start!
Millionaires don't work 10 hours a week!
I know very few millionaires who work part-time on their businesses.
In fact, I know very few people who do.
Success and income give freedom to spend time doing things you love.
Successful professional artists typically love what they're doing.
Behind studio doors, they're eating, sleeping, and breathing their business.
Competitive, driven, over-achiever is a key to growth and success.
However they play, successful professional artists also work hard!

Do you have what it takes?
If not what are you going to do?

Do you remember how you learned to drive?
There was learning how to parallel park.
These days there are cars that do that, themselves!
Then what about the frustration of learning to drive a manual car?
You stalled so many times you never got out of the parking lot.
And you failed your license test anyway – just like I did!

But then you finally pass and get your license.
Remember the freedom the first time you took the wheel by yourself?
You went car out for a spin - there's nothing quite like it.

Learning to drive is hard to learn, but once you do, it's easy.
Learning how to make money as an artist is like that too.
It can be frustrating.
You make painfully slow progress trying to build a reliable income.

You will be overwhelmed by the amount of work you do daily.
You have to paint many more works than previously.
But then there's the business part too.
Otherwise there is **NO** money!

What if you have to juggle building a career while working a day job?
But it doesn't have to be like that!
All of this can change in a very short period of time.
You can be on your way to driving your career freely starting right away.
All you have to do is start learning how.

But where will you actually start?
Most people think an exhibition is the beginning of a professional career.
Artists even think this.
Was driving on a long journey what you did first when you got your licence?

But before we get to that what happens to those old works?
What happens to your past and that's what your old works are – the past!

You want to move to a career, as a well-known and successful artist.
So what will those works that belong to your past do now?
Nothing except undermine your new status.
You must distance yourself from those works.

The best way is to do it publicly and dramatically.
Find all your old paintings – the lot.
You no longer need them as insurance in case something goes wrong.
You have a momentum going with your work and they are not part of it.

Before your FIRST exhibition sort out paintings sketches and prints.

Keep these ones:
Those that represent your new way.
Those that you intend to keep and not sell (perhaps your superannuation).
Very good frames in sizes you can re-use (not the painting but the frame).
Stuff you give away (relevant to new works, some prints) in promotions.

Your paintings now are the equivalent of actual cash.
So most of the old ones can't be given away.

To maintain the cash value of your works all must be your best.
So look carefully at those old works.
Are there any as good as the latest works?
If you are really sure about that then put them aside.

All the rest get burnt.
Burn most prints to increase dramatically an edition being "sold out".
In future do not print anything like that number.

But be quite objective and single-minded about this.

Your future depends on not letting a single work out.
That's not to your latest standard.

Now let the party begin.
Have a party where you live.
Invite your neighbours as well as the press.
Take those lesser works out into your front yard, or street if necessary.
Choose a fine week-end morning when there will be plenty of people about.

BURN them along with warped and damaged stretchers and frames.
Burn each work and frame one at a time.
That takes longer and is more spectacular.
Dress suitably but **NOT** weird.
For you are a responsible and sensible artist.

Hold up each work dramatically for all to see then throw it on the fire.
Pretend you are a priest of some obscure faith.

Each sacrifice is accompanied by a ritual.
If asked for your fire permit – reply by telling them what you are doing.
You are celebrating your turning point as an artist by burning your past.

Tell them about your upcoming exhibition.
Give them a catalogue for your next exhibition.
Set up a table so you can sign the catalogues.
Invite people to your opening reception.

If the police come because of the fire.
Tell them what you are doing, and invite them too.
If they want one free – refuse.

When the fire burns out, sweep up the ashes.
Put them in a container you have brought.

Gather your table and the exhibition catalogues and move to your house.
Without a glance backward wave to those still gathered at the scene.

Your exhibition will be a success.
You are now on your way to being famous.
Years ago I read in the national papers of an Australian artist.
He did something similar, he certainly burnt his old works.
I was just an art student at that time.
So although I remember the event my recollection of the details is sketchy.
Not like they would be now.

The important thing is, I've never forgotten this either.
Almost all works have magical properties due to the creative process.
Use this common myth to your advantage to embark on your new career.

Could you make a dramatic statement like this?
Where would that take your new career?

What qualification is required to be a professional?
Becoming a professional comes in one of two quite different ways.

One is possessing qualifications, related to professional training.
Like doctors, teachers, accountants, nurses, butchers, and so on.
They all possess qualifications gained by study and passing courses.

They can't practice as professionals without qualification.
Even then, further training on the job may be needed.
Then the new practitioner can become established, as a professional.

But tennis players, golfers, gamblers, and many others, are different.
They are able to practice their profession right from the start.

It's whether they get paid that determines their professionalism.
That is decided by how they perform.

Even this group is similar to the first.
They practice, improve, attend clinics with coaches to develop their skills.
The hobbyist just enjoys the activity.

So you can see it is education that makes a professional.
Whatever its kind.

It could be either a formal education or an informal one.
The professional acquires skills, knowledge and attitudes.
These include business knowledge related to their activity.
That sets them apart from a hobby or amateur in the same field.

The professional knows they must do 'the hard yards' in training.
Include the business aspects.
Otherwise they'll never be able to perform consistently at a high level.

Sport illustrates those attitudes.
A professional tennis player spends hours daily on one aspect of his game.
They'll also spend a great deal of time in the gym.
Developing specific strengths an addition to general high level fitness.

They will have a coach, perhaps even several.
Most time is spent thinking about, practicing and performing their sport.

Even with a professional approach there are no guarantees.
Because sport is competitive and there are winners and losers.
But the individual professional makes the most of their natural talent.

Money is often a measure of relative performances.
No matter what kind of education money measures success.
Roger Federer has earned much more than I have from tennis, for example.

In art it's no different.
Paper qualification, should mean an acquisition of suitable knowledge.
They should also develop appropriate skills, and a professional attitude.
An artist continues from these 'starting blocks' to become a professional.
It's possible to gain all these things without any 'paper' qualification.
Where this happens, such a person can be a professional too.

But can you make a living from art?

Often we start as a local artist.
People buy your work for it's what they want and they have no alternatives.
But you can only lack alternatives if you live where no other artist does.
We have to appear as clearly different from others who seem competitive.
If we manage this, then they're no longer competitors.

So we can position ourselves as THE local artist.
ALL of our works are of local subjects.
Paint readily identifiable area landmarks.
Become the Black Rock, or wherever, artist.
Paint local works for visiting dignitaries to receive, and be publicized for it.
The idea is that when anyone thinks local art, they think of you.

Your signature could, even should, set you apart.
We recognise 'Vincent', and many other artists, by their style or subject.

AND their signature.
Without the signature there is doubt about the authenticity of the work.
Promote your signature so people recognise it easily.
It's all part of positioning yourself as an artist.

Your aim should be to grow your artist business.
Show your clients you are serious about your career and confident too.
So provide a money back guarantee if they're not satisfied.
This will generate extra sales, quite apart from showing confidence.

Would you like to make not just a living, but a very good living?
There are artists who do this, but most don't.
It's not the art that makes the difference, but the attitude.
Same goes for making a really good living from teaching art.

Some time ago I read an old car magazine (one of my other interests).
I came across a story that I thought would appeal to you.
It's about Alistair Brookham (p70 - 72, 'Sports Driver', issue 6 1990).
Alistair makes model cars for a living!

In fact he makes model racing and sports cars, not just any car
But before he started he raced cars, and was a mechanical draftsman too.
So he did have a good background.
In addition his father was a model-maker, although not professionally.
He knew what workmanship, enthusiasm and dedication achieved.
He made a number of decisions before starting his model-making career.

He had to decide which car to build (yes which ONE).
He also had to consider where he could find buyers.
How much they would be prepared to pay.
Not how much he wanted – well not then anyway.
Back in 1982 he started by building two models.
He chose Ferrari racing cars for he was sure there'd be some interest.

Before picking up any tools, Alistair did a huge amount of research.
He studied books and every available drawing and photograph.
He has a large library these days.
Following exhaustive research and relying on his drafting background.
Alistair draws every component to the exact size that he will make them.

This is not easy as he is mainly working from photographs.
They may not show accurate measurements due to distortion.
That means, sometimes he has to make a part several times to get it right!

Alistair spends about two months on the design aspect.
He draws each part in the order he will assemble them.
He works from seven in the morning until around nine at night.
These days he usually builds five cars a year!
Not going into details, Alistair estimates it takes 800 hours to build a model.

He worked part time on those first two Ferraris, for three months.
However it became obvious that he would have to make it full time.
So his modelling career depended on the success of those first two cars.
They were sold, but there were no repeat sales or even enquiries.
So it was back to the drafting board for Alastair.

In 1986 (4 years later), a sports car magazine ran an article.
On Alistair's cars and the subsequent interest set the ball rolling again.
The demand for his work is now considerable.

When I read the article he had enough work for the next ten years.
Alistair asks for a considerable deposit and expects cash prior to delivery.
His clients range from museums to investors and enthusiasts.
One thing they have in common is an ability to pay a high price tag.
It's a price that relates to the time, effort and skill that has gone into the car.

There's a message here for you whether as an artist or teacher.
The better background you have the greater your chance of success.
But even with this you still need the professional attitude.

Right from the start Alastair was focused on his potential clients.
He didn't leave sales to chance.

How much research do you do?
Alastair does a great deal of research before starting.
Are there black and white studies, colour sketches, and small trial pieces?
There are artists who do this for each work that becomes a print.

Most artists merely toss off a work and expect people to pay for it.
They expect people will pay because the artist has produced the work.
That's even though it was done to meet their personal creative needs.
Such an attitude is amateurish and doesn't deserve any encouragement.

Perhaps there's no need to put in 800 hours on a painting?
Or work full time and do only five per year!
But imagine what you'd produce if you did?

Analyze your approach to your work.
Which means you can work out whether you are truly a professional artist.
Can your teaching meet the same criteria?
What about your artworks could they be exhibited?

What sort of exhibition would you want anyway?
Most exhibitions sell just one or two works.
Many sell none but do you want an exhibition like those?

Why do most exhibitions fail?
Perhaps the works were not 'good' enough?
That's generally what the gallery thinks so that could be true.
It's also what visitors to the gallery think!
Are yours?

To make sure of a successful exhibition you produce excellent works!
Then you will not share the fate of those other artists will you?
But what if you do?

Could it be that the gallery doesn't really know much about selling?
They provide space, lighting and access to people at a party.

But is this enough?
Clearly in most cases it is NOT.
So there might be some truth in a gallery not knowing its business.
Should you have your work at galleries like that?

How can you tell a good gallery from a poor one anyway?
Basically there are two types of galleries.
There are those who are willing to provide exhibition space for you.
There are those who are not.

The first galleries want new artists.
That's because they are **NOT** selling enough works by the ones they have.
Their business strategy is to keep supplying new works for their prospects.
Eventually they hope some actually sell.
They'll also want you to supply 45 works!

The galleries who do not want your work are quite different.
They **ARE** selling works by the artists they have.

Their commitment is to them.
If you join their team it will be to you too and that's where you want to be!
OK so you know what sort of gallery you don't want.
You also know what sort of exhibition you don't want.

Well what sort DO you want?
Obviously a sell-out exhibition is the best possible result.
They **DO** happen **AND** people remember them **AND** talk about them too.

Maybe those artists are really good artists?

Or do they happen just because of luck?

Or is it someone knows what they are doing and creates such a result?

Perhaps an exhibition isn't the beginning of a professional career?
It's just the public announcement.
A lot happens before that to make the result not just possible but inevitable!
The burning strategy could be a prelude to your first exhibition.

A decision to become a professional artist is the first step.
You then need to learn all the things needed for success.
Learning how to sell while prices are still very low is one of those things.

Improving your productivity is also important.
The more works you produce the more income you can potentially earn.
But this will not need to be at the expense of your style or focus.

There are other things you need to know about too.
All this will take considerable time.
It might be best to continue juggling a career and working a day job?
But you are now becoming a professional artist as well.
You no longer paint just for enjoyment **BUT** it is also to earn money.

Eventually at your first exhibition you pull out all stops to sell the lot.
You only get one chance to do this!
If your preparation is right it can happen.
BUT people WILL remember it for a long time.
Underscore their memory at the end of the exhibition.
Have another burning of older works but not frames that you can use.

What are the things needed for success?
List all those things.

Painting in any size is essential for the professional artist.

That ability provides pricing options other artists can only envy.

Establish a clear price/size relationship in people's minds.

Mix combinations over the years and steadily work up the price scale.

You'll also need to modify the numbers of a particular size that are for sale.

Here's an illustration:

Gallery 1 is a new venue, not previously exhibited at.

Gallery 3 is one where a strong following has been built up.

Gallery 2 is in between.

A, B, C, D, and E are different sizes (see next page).

YEAR	GALLERY 1	GALLERY 2	GALLERY 3
1	10 X A @ $250	10 X A @ $250	5 X B @ $500
	5 X B @ $500	5 X C @ $850	5 X C @ $850
	5 X C @ $850	5 X D @ $1200	5 X D @ $1200
			5 X E @ $1500
YEAR	GALLERY 1	GALLERY 2	GALLERY 3
2	10 X A @ $350	5 X B @ $500	10 X B @ $500
	5 X C @ $900	10 X C @ $900	5 X D @ $1200
	5 X D @ $1200	5 X D @ $1200	5 X E @ $1800
YEAR	GALLERY 1	GALLERY 2	GALLERY 3
3	5 X A @ $400	5 X B @ $650	5 X B @ $650
	5 X B @ $650	5 X C @ $950	5 X C @ $950
	5 X C @ $950	5 X D @ $1500	5 X D @ $1500
	5 X D @ $1500	5 X E @ $1900	5 X E @ $1900
YEAR	GALLERY 1	GALLERY 2	GALLERY 3
4	10 X B @ $750	5 X B @ $750	5 X C @ $1200
	5 X C @ $1200	10 X C @ $1200	5 X D @ $1600
	5 X D @ $1600	5 X D @ $1600	10X E @ $1950

In another year all galleries will be at much the same level of return.

In this example the price for each size is the same at each venue.

There might be a lower price for a certain size at Gallery 1 than Gallery 2.

And particularly Gallery 3.

This is especially in first few years, whilst getting established in Gallery 1.

Notice the pricing effect at the $500, $1000 and $2000 thresholds.

Hold prices under these levels for longer than you might logically.

When you go over skip more than would be logical for even steps.

Here's where you make up for holding the price down.

But you will not be able to implement these pricing strategies.

Unless you can control the size of your works!

That is an essential skill for the professional artist.

3. Framing is dressing up the work.

A framed work is more appealing than the same work unframed.
From a commercial angle, this is more important than many artists think.
An inappropriate frame can cost you sales.

There are two common framing mistakes.
Underplay framing and not provide the visual support a work deserves.
This happens when an artist stops thinking when they finished the painting.

But extravagant 'over the top' framing is an error too.
That takes attention from the work.
Often picture framers' are responsible for this kind of expensive mistake.

People select works visually, and a part of what they see is the frame.
They do not usually distinguish the framing from the work.
They look at the total package.

Intelligent framing increases the chance of a buyer.
So if your work is pretty awful, you'll need a frame that disguises this fact.
Obviously a frame that calls attention to itself will do the trick.

But better still save your money.
Paint over the work and don't worry about selling until you have improved.

Attention getting frames reduce the effect of the work itself.
Most artists realize this, and frame so it doesn't unduly call attention to itself.
BUT it's better if the frame harmonizes with and enhances the work.
Then your framing is likely to assist the sales campaign.

Artists have a problem when choosing frames for their own work.
They do not usually know who is going to buy them.

But for a commission you can consider the buyer's tastes.
You do want them to buy don't you?
You're not changing your work, only the package.

So by selecting the 'right' frame it's possible to increase your sales.
Right doesn't just mean right for the work, it also means right for the client.
Imagine the sort of person who'll buy your painting?

That's the point of packaging – it is marketing.
It's a way of making the goods (paintings) appeal to the market.
Use fashionable frames for a decorative office market if your works appeal.
Similarly gold leaf is almost mandatory in offices on high priced paintings.
This kind of framing supports the work in its intended market.
Can you imagine a Rolls Royce without leather seats?

So imagine the sort of environment in which they'll hang the work.
A painting in a mansion looks different from one in modest circumstances.
A frame for a painting for a bedroom is different than one for the lounge.

You need some understanding of the psychology of the client.
Don't worry if you don't know much, use whatever knowledge you have.
Select a frame they'd like and which will fit in their environment.

This isn't quite the same as selecting framing you like.
But the more you try, the better you'll get.

What if you're unsure about which actual frame to choose for a work?
Gold is the safest option (silver the least safe) as it gives a luxury look.
Any extra cost is small when stacked up against the probability of sales.

How important is size?

Is there a correlation between size and cost?
Most beginning artists are aware of a relationship between size and cost.
That's why they usually paint small paintings.
Often their teachers exhort them to work larger and 'free up'.

It's difficult to 'free up' if you are worried about cost of the materials.
The most obvious costs are for frames, stretchers, canvas or paper.

But there's also the cost in time.
Bigger works take far longer to complete than small ones.
This leads to a productivity cost.
In any given time more small works can be produced than larger ones.
For a beginner that's a better pathway to help free up than few larger works.

Is there value in smaller works?
A small work doesn't cost too much to frame, even elaborately.
However, the frame cost proportion of any selling price is quite high.
This reduces considerably the return on small works.
It can make selling small works uneconomical, except in high volumes.
But that is difficult for a fledgling artist to achieve anyway.

What is done depends on a time/cost balance related to production.
There's still value in small works, even if a frame reduces the return.
Small paintings can be used to open up a market for your work.
Once that has been done the size and prices can be increased.
Then you start to reap a better reward for your efforts.

Controlling size is how professional and leisure artists differ.
So can you control the size of a work?
Obviously if you can then you control your major costs of production.
It's actually quite easy.
Just control the size of canvas, paper, board, plate or what you work on.
That determines the size of your work before you even start!

Similar sized works mean you make cost effective framing choices.
Quite obviously you can re-use frames.

Paint to a standard size (you decide what).
Then all your works are that size.

They fit the same sized frame and you do not have to frame all.
Just some.
The works can be swapped in frames, with more frames as sales happen.
Thus ten works may only cost you three or four frames to start with.

A development is standardize the sizes of your frames.
I have four major frame sizes, each of which is ½ or 2x the size of another.
Occasionally I paint even larger work, which is still in the same proportion.
I don't have many spare frames, even though I have unsold unframed work.

If works are the same size only a few need to be framed.
The works can be rotated in the frames from time to time.
Then it is possible to provide unframed works to galleries.
Supply fewer frames so they swap them about as they show work to clients.
This way a gallery can have a good supply of your paintings.
But you don't have to spend too much on framing (or freight).

After a while you can even standardize frame styles.
You'll discover which frames look the best and sell the best too.
You have works in a number of places, presented well in optimum sizes.
But they haven't cost you any more than necessary for framing.

Most artists relate their prices to different sizes.
It also happens in most other fields.
You pay more for a large car by a manufacturer, than a smaller one.

A bigger house always costs more than a smaller one of similar standard.
So it should be for your artwork.

If you hire out artworks then the same principle should be followed.
The larger works cost more to hire than smaller works.
They also take more wall space so you'll hire fewer.
Again this is what people expect.

If hired works are from other artists reframing is an expensive option.
In this case just group the works within (say) five size ranges.
Call them very large, large, medium, small or miniature size.

Again this is what people expect.
In addition the larger works occupy more wall space than smaller works.
Thus opportunities for additional sales/hiring are lost.

With hired works the sizes also determine the hire fees payable.
If you are selling then the size influences the retail price.

Do not put inferior works on hire (or sale) at any price!
You will regret it down the track if you don't take this seemingly drastic step.
Don't even give them away.
Even some of what you consider good works will come back to haunt you.

Well what about the really good works you may now say?
There will always be some paintings you prefer over others.
But other people's choices will usually be different.
If this wasn't the case, you'd only sell the works you really like!

People hire what they like, not what you like.
Price it (or them) the same as other works the same size.
Otherwise do not offer them for rent at all, keep and enjoy these yourself.

It is hard to hire works with no clear correlation between fee and size.
This is particularly so at higher price levels.
You are sending signals the work is not consistent and the quality varies.
People become confused if their choice is a lower price than it should be.
They tend to back off.
Check hire works for quality and remove those not up to the mark.

Which means others can be priced according to their sizes and media also.

Frame colour influences sales.

Selection of artwork for its colour is mostly at low price levels.
It's a component in decorating so a decorator is more likely to buy prints.
They're cheaper and in a big choice of subjects and colour combinations.
It's much more likely they'll find what they're after, too.

If you sell to this market work in different colour combinations.
Read decoration and trade magazines for ideas on what is 'hot'.
Generally harmonious combinations are popular.

At the subconscious level colour has an effect too.
This psychology influences buying artworks not selected as decoration.
The decore market is also subject to the same psychological influences.
For example, warmer colours have more appeal than cooler hues.
Test this at a gallery - are there many green or blue paintings?

Colour and design is a major field of study.
It's primarily about understanding and applying these psychological factors.
These issues are relevant to framing, and matboard choices.
As they are also to the colour used by you in your actual works.

When framing select the mat or slip before you select the moulding.
In other words when designing a frame work out from the artwork itself.
A wide component (mat, slip, frame) has a major visual impact.
Tone (lightness, darkness) is an important link between a work and frame.

When I had a picture framing business I wanted unique frames.
Raw wooden frames offer artists and framers a wide variety of options.

Stains and finishes create various appearances from the same moulding. Timber frames can be on artworks from contemporary to tradition styles. They can also be appropriate for many interior design schemes.

Don't make a common mistake using special timbers or finishes.
The frame competes for attention with the artwork.
You are not likely to do this but a framer might.
But for you there's a chance the frame doesn't complement the work.
This also is a mistake as a buyer pays money for a complete package.
The frame and the work must look right and be in harmony for a sale.

Wooden moulding can range from inexpensive to quite costly.
Use timbers in quality furniture like mahogany, rosewood, oak, or walnut.
There is a richness of colour and texture which underpin furniture use.
So they convey a quality appearance when used as a frame.

Warping can be a major problem for anyone using timber.
This is a particular difficulty for an artist doing their own framing.

You will not make the volume of frames that even a small framer does.
So it is likely moulding spends a long time in storage before being used.
The risk of warped moulding is enhanced by time.

The best counter is buy small quantities, even though this costs more.
One warped stick costs the price of the piece of moulding.
Another counter is to make up frames in advance of the need.
If you have a small range of frame sizes for your works this is a good thing.
You are ready for an instant exhibition for example.

The warping danger means storage conditions are critical.
Air conditioned storage is best as is warmth in winter.
Buy moulding lengths that have been milled, dried and stored properly.
Most are like this as the suppliers do not want returns of warped moulding.

Do you change frames?

Are you willing to change the frame on a work?
If so you can make the critical breakthrough that leads to a sale.

When I had a gallery one artist always had plain limed timber frames.
He liked the simplicity and understated effect.
Unfortunately few of his clients shared his taste.
We found that when a gold frame was substituted, sales rose.
The works also presented in an enhanced manner.

So framing does make a difference to sales.
Primarily because people are buying the package.
Clients usually do not have the experience of an artist or gallery person.
So they don't mentally separate the frame from the work aesthetically.

If a potential buyer doesn't like the whole package.
There's no analysis regarding why that is so, they just move to a next work.

Yes, framing is expensive and for most artists their major cost as well.
If you paint in a standard range of sizes.
Frames can be swapped from one work to another eventually all are sold.

Thus using more expensive moulding might be an initial burden.
But it's one that's eventually recouped.

But what if the client does want the frame changed?
In most cases, they want a style of frame that you do not usually use.
Deal with people who want to have special fancy frames.
On their new (or contemplated) purchase like this.
Tell them you have chosen simple frames so they can take it to their framer.
Then get exactly what they want, without paying for the frame already there.

Georgeann Waggaman (Colorado, USA) does this.

Do you have trouble with your framing?
Perhaps you need a policy so you know what to do in any situation?

4. Success is an upward spiral.

Becoming a professional artist.
Involves many things about which I know nothing.

For example do you earn an income by doing something now?
Will you still earn that when you become a professional artist?
Can you earn a part-time income?
Do you have sufficient savings to live on for say a year (at least)?
Is there another bread-winner in the family or are you wealthy?
These questions need to be asked and answered so you know what to do.

What will family think, particularly when you spend days painting?
They think you are having fun but you think you are a professional artist!
What happens if it takes a while (a year or more) to actually earn money?
It will take still longer to make a living.
Will you be able to keep the family's support that long?
Will you be able to maintain your own motivation in those circumstances?

Are you ready for the business side of the profession?
That will in the end determine whether you are successful or not.

Great paintings do not necessarily sell.
Can you handle it when that happens, repeatedly?
Just selling a few paintings is not sufficient to make a living from.
You have to sell hundreds!

As a professional merely painting well is not sufficient.
Most professionals do that!
For the first couple of years you will be learning your profession.
So you should ask yourself, if you really want to do this?
You also need to be successful as a business and that's different!

Better to waste a few dollars with something from me you don't use.

Than a whole lot of time involved in a profession you really shouldn't be in.

Now is when to think seriously about the venture you are considering.

If you want to be a professional artist then you must do the job properly.

I mean really back yourself, with no half-measures!

Maybe you might make some concessions to the market from time to time.

Particularly as you set up your career.

It will take time and money.

This means your time and your money.

You can't doubt yourself or you'll fail!

Just forget all ideas of failure or quit now!

Neither is it likely that you will sell enough works to live from.

Eventually that can happen, but not straight away.

BUT if you wait until Christmas, next year, the 'right' time.

All that happens is the whole process has been delayed.

There needs to be much work actually done, before there is any return.

A start must be made, if time is available, before any income is earned.

Other projects are foregone, delayed, accelerated to begin a career.

If you are to be successful then you need to be professional!

How will you know you are a success?

But consider these comments:

'Strong self-discipline and intelligent self-management are in my view the fundamental building blocks for all success.' (p77)

There will be disappointments along the way, that's how we learn. Each disappointment is a test of your commitment. They also add to your experience and strength. In the end your commitment is the key to your success. (Don Talbot Australian swimming coach in "Nothing but the best")

I have written that there is no short cut to success.

This applies in art as in other areas.

This might sound depressing.

So you could wonder whether you should even bother trying!

But it's just one side of a coin and it doesn't mean success is unattainable.

Success is attainable as there are successful artists and you can be one.

Success is related to time.

Time has an effect on what we do and shows itself obviously in our learning.

If we have learned something we do not usually forget it.

If we learn something we can build on that in ways not previously seen.

But we have to start with that initial learning.

But instead of building new sets of ideas we can just repeat the old ones.

That is a choice we have.

But relatively small ideas can become altered.

That's when the context changes or they are associated with other ideas.

As you paint one work do you think of others that could be done?

Are they not developments from that initial work?

Wasn't that a development from earlier works too?

Most people have heard of the downward spiral or vicious circle.

Here negative momentum is the driving force.

The poor get poorer, have more children, lose their jobs or can't get a job.

It seems to be a never-ending spiral and only a few escape!

But on the other hand there are upward spiral too.

This is where things start in a small and insignificant way.

They gradually build and increase in momentum.

As they link with an increasing number of other ideas.

Ideas can thus spiral upwards, so they almost seem to be self-sufficient.

This upwards spiral is integral to the creative process.

It also provides the momentum leading to success.

There is no short cut but there is a spiral which you can climb aboard.

That happens if you focus on maintaining momentum not getting to the end.

It's more important to be ever more successful than to achieve success.

Even with small steps the former attitude will lead to the latter attainment.

Upward spirals can be powerful.
They seem to fuel themselves and become self-propelling in time.
Successful people get more chances to be even more successful.
Those who need opportunities never seem to get one!
Many people think this is luck, either good or bad depending on its nature.

But this isn't luck.
Upward spirals are everywhere and can be harnessed by an alert person.
That's how we make our own luck.

Good ideas can come from anywhere.
It's up to you to notice and be open to them.
But you also need to harness them to your advantage.
They can be good painting ideas.
But career ideas are also subject to the same forces.

This momentum can accompany a career.
Spirals build slowly but gradually gain momentum.
Other spirals interlock and momentum gathers more rapidly.
In time success is attained.
But there is no short cut.

Word of mouth is an upward spiral working for your career.

Do you have career transition strategies?
OK you are ready to become a full-time artist.
It's a wonderful career and certainly worth aspiring towards.
But how are you going to do it?
Keep doing what you have been up until now; but with more time?

Will that get you there?

How can you be sure?

Well maybe you'll do what you see other artists doing?

But if that's what you do you're likely to obtain similar results to them.

This is pretty scary for many people, so they put off taking the plunge.

They wait for the right time, which never comes!

There is no right time, other when you say let's do it now.

On the other hand you can look at your new career as a challenge.

This is probably the better way, for it surely will be.

Just what is the challenge that confronts you?

It's not just to start a professional art career is it?

But the real challenge is to be successful!

So what does this mean to you?

Whatever that is only happens if you make it happen which takes planning.

Initially strategic (long term) planning is required.

You have to know where exactly you want to get to in (say) five years.

In that period of time someone can become a Ph. D.

Can you be the art career equivalent?

You won't need to go to university and study what they teach there.

But you do need the same qualities of character as the university graduate.

I'll mention some shortly, but they are totally dedicated to their objective.

Can you have that kind of commitment to achieving your goals?

So at the start decide where you'd like to be in five years' time.

Imagine that it's happened and you are looking back on the past five years.

Just what have you achieved?

What can you do now that you couldn't when you started?

Make a list of all those things.

Be specific.
Just saying you can make a living by selling your paintings is not enough.
That's just a dream.

How much is your annual income (now)?
How many works do you sell?
What are their prices (on average)?
Where do you sell them?
What kind of works are they?
What sorts of people buy your work?
Do you sell through galleries or elsewhere?
Which galleries, how busy are you - get the idea?

Now this isn't what is happening now is it?
If that was the case then you need to think again about your future.
Or you are totally satisfied and need read no further.

So what exactly do you need to do to achieve those goals?
Write down what you have to do.
Your goals will guide your thinking.
Do whatever is necessary to head in that direction.
Don't begin things that take from that for they'll only waste precious time.

For example you'll have works in seven galleries in three years.
But right now you have none anywhere.
Obviously you'll do things so your work is accepted by the gallery people.
There's a great deal of thought and planning required.

The first thing you should ask yourself is, are you good enough?
If you're not, then there's no point starting.
Fortunately it's only you who has to think you are god enough!
It's hard for the best artists but impossible for those not up to standard.
If that's your situation, just put your head down.

Get "brush mileage" until you are good enough to look seriously at a career.

But let's say you don't have that problem.
There are many excellent hobby artists, and you might be one of them.
This won't guarantee success though.
But it is the bare minimum for starting down the career pathway.
OK what do you do first?

You could just go to a gallery, and show them your work.
You're likely to get the same result as other artists which is rejection.
Perhaps you could send a carefully prepared portfolio with your best work?
Same result.
What you need to do it is sit down and think very carefully.
Gaining gallery representation is a key step in developing your career.
It's too important to muck up and elsewhere I'll develop this theme.
One suggestion is to visit several galleries.
Ask them what someone like you should do, and then do it!

Moving from where you are now to where you'd like to be in the future.
Requires continuous learning.
By asking those galleries you'll learn something.

By testing that out at one gallery you'll learn more.
Keep learning and you'll keep improving and eventually will be rewarded.
You now have a glimpse of character a Ph. D. student demonstrates.
But which you need too.
Here are some of the key traits needed for success with your art career:

Perseverance and persistence:
Without this nothing will happen.

You've probably heard that 'faint heart never won fair lady'.

Your art career will not happen either unless you stick at it too.
Staying power to keep you going when times get tough is essential.
For there will be tough times.
This quality can even make up for deficiencies in other areas.

Self-confidence:
You must believe in yourself.
You must feel you can overcome obstacle and barriers.
Otherwise you'll give up at the first hurdle.
Without self-confidence you'll always be shackled by doubts.

Enthusiasm:
Enthusiasm provides the drive necessary to overcome those hurdles.
You'll be able to visualize a greater number of opportunities you can tackle.
It also generates a positivity that attracts people to your cause.
Belief:
You must believe in the worth of what you are doing.
This isn't just your painting but also the idea of a full-time professional artist.

Often people don't really believe it is a worthwhile pursuit.
They'll fail of course'
What we believe influences thoughts and actions and outcomes of plans.
Those who believe they have reached their limit have and coast from there.

Yes luck never went astray.
Luck is a willingness to discern opportunities and take advantage of them.
It's closely linked to optimism.

Being concerned:
Being concerned is different from worrying.
Worry is a sense of fear that paralyses action.
Concern is a realistic understanding that problems are likely.

Concern lets you prepare for challenges before they become significant.

Flexibility:
Sometimes it's important to be able to change direction.
Unexpected opportunities may arise and if not taken will be lost forever.
One the other hand sometime things do not work out as expected.

We need to adjust some element and try again.
Or perhaps that action should be put aside for the moment.
Not always will we attempt things at the most opportune time.

Failure coping:
Problems are not failures but temporary setbacks from which we can learn.
You are better able to deal with setbacks that inevitably comes along.
Particularly if you analyze what happened and learn from the experience.
OK think carefully about whether you are good enough?
If so then start developing those career transition strategies!

Should you go to art school?
Does going to art school guarantee your success as an artist?
It's a way into a career as a professional artist and I did this myself once.
I'm still not sure whether I've made it into the professional artist ranks.
I think I may have entered an entirely different career altogether.

The chances of success in the art world are actually extremely small.
Australia has about 50 art schools with 50 or so graduates annually.
Even if they didn't intend to become one, most are contemporary artists.
For that's what is taught!

There are 10 to 20 contemporary galleries in Melbourne or Sydney.
With perhaps a dozen exhibiting artists each.
But quite a few of these galleries are struggling financially.
It's the same in other countries too.

The chances are therefore stacked against you.
You might be one of the three or four graduates.
Who gain quality commercial representation straight out of art school.
Even then it will probably take ten to 15 years to become self-sufficient.

That's if you are lucky.
But by that time the numbers will have reduced considerably.

Most graduates will no longer be practicing by then.
So hang in there and eventually you could be successful.
One wonders, with this scenario, how art schools justify their existence!
Going to art school may well extinguish any natural talent you already have.
Particularly if your aspirations are to work in a more conventional manner.
So it would be unwise to go into debt just to find that out.

Art school is also about becoming socialized in the art world.
You learn the conventional wisdom of how things function in artist's world.

Unfortunately that is also the path followed by most artists.
They are not successful!
So perhaps there is no real need to learn that stuff?

But, what if you want to know about the latest philosophical theories?
You could learn such things if you go to the right school.
Look for an art school that has theory and its application in the visual arts.
If it is attached to a university, then you can use that degree later on.
But perhaps you may be better off actually studying philosophy?

Why do you want to go to art school?
Answer that question and you'll start to know whether you should.

5. Conclusion

Take a realistic and long-term approach to the artistic profession.
Money from art can come with patience, persistence and determination.
The stories of artists who spent years struggling are common (van Gogh).
Many got there in the end (not van Gogh).

It is the first step that is difficult.
Do you have the financial resources to keep going?
AND believe in yourself enough?

Will you be battling for a gallery?
I was a gallery owner (1979 to the end of 1997), and I am also an artist.
Most artists are not going to receive much satisfaction from galleries.

Most gallery owners don't know about selling nor marketing either.
Most do what they think other galleries do.
Artists have little knowledge either.
I was one of them but learned what to do by making mistakes.

Not all gallery owners resist new ideas.
Most are battling just like artists.
So they are willing to co-operate with any artist to get a better result.

It's possibly better to have your own gallery as many artists do.
Then there is total control.
An artist selling from his studio can do most of the same things as a gallery.
This is the future for artists who must depend on their own efforts.

Certainly you should be in no hurry to quit your day job!
Demand is not even close to matching supply of artworks.
That's the main reason most artwork is never sold, but gathers dust.

But you can't get into any business without finance!
You can't stay in business without finance and an artist is no different.
If you can't find money to frame a work you can't finance a mail campaign.

In fact they can't finance even Preparation Tools (this book).
If you can't afford to frame paintings you can't be a professional artist.
Spend time raising finance from which to launch and sustain a career.
Certainly you should be in no hurry to quit your day job!

Many begin a career as a professional artist, or contemplate it.
But it's **NOT** artistic skills that decide success.
Without these skills you shouldn't be trying to make a professional career.
Many artists do have those skills and are still not successful.
Professionalism is required for success in any field, including an artist.

An important message if you are the starting gates of a career.
The odds are stacked against success.
That's because of all the paintings ever painted, most are **NEVER** sold!

The main problem really is there are not enough buyers!
The art industry is a depressed industry.
That means there is an oversupply compared to consumption.

All the unsold works are a testament to this situation.
They are lying in studios and galleries waiting for a buyer.
In many cases the artist has even given up on trying to sell them.
So they are just stored.

This doesn't mean you can't make it.
BUT you must very organized and clear headed about what you are doing.
You battle all manner of alternative ways someone can spend their $.
You need determination, courage, persistence, imagination, planning.

AND help.

BUT the good news is it can be done!
There are artists who do make a living and you can join their ranks.
But you will need to take the tough professional route.

OK you can paint well so what about making money?
But being a professional artist requires something extra.
Your artwork doesn't sell itself In spite of a widely held belief it does.
If it did, you'd be able to hang your work anywhere and people would buy.

You've learnt how to sell and have a list of prospects and buyers.
You've created a simple website as a way to help develop your contact list.
You also understand pricing and know the importance of framing.

With all that in place your career foundation has been laid!
BUT if you do **NOT** have **ALL** those preliminary steps in place.
Your career will **NOT** be as successful as you would like.
For example exhibition sales will probably **NOT** happen.

The world does not owe even a single artist a living, you must earn it.
Your income will **NOT** compound as prices rise with additional sales.
You'll get very few referrals to increase the number of works you can sell.
There will be stagnation or even a decline!
You may even have experienced good sales in the past.
However that doesn't mean they will continue now.

Your income is linked to the artworks you produce AND sell!
NO artworks sold = NO money.
You need to earn income in sufficient amounts to live the life you want.

The world has changed in the last few years.

There is less discretionary income so new things need to be done.
The number of works other artists do during a year affects you too.
They are competing with you for whatever sales there are.

Where do you sell your stuff anyway?
If you have a gallery or studio that can cater for visitors that is a possibility.

But what if you don't then what can you do?
Sell from empty shops.
Real estate people prefer to have you there than have the shop empty.
You'd be surprised at the deal you might be able to negotiate.
You do not need to use all the shop, just the part closest to the street.
Even just using the window front might be suitable!

Use a website to sell at other people's homes and places of business.
Email images people are interested in, or they view them on your website.
You can have a client view your website and talk to you at the same time,
Some of the latest technology makes this possible and is quite cheap.
You can both look at the website and be on the phone too if necessary.
Then bring the prospect's selection for them to view at their office or home.

It is possible to hold an Open Studio in conjunction with other artists.
Your Christmas event could be promoted concurrently.
But you need to do an independent promotion and offer special discounts.
A description that stands out from all the other artists is necessary.
You want to attract buying visitors rather than people just on an art tour.

Attend Christmas Fairs, Art and Craft shows at different times.
Then it is possible to have your special exhibition at multiple outlets.

You must give your display a special twist to stand out from the competition.

Seasonally themed decorations are an obvious way to go.

You might be able to sell at one show and deliver at a later one.

Your own house can be used.

Just take one room, which is at or near your entrance and away you go.

This idea all depends on where you live and who is likely to attend.

Former buyers or people who previously expressed interest reduce risk.

Your own studio is similar to having the exhibition at your own house.

You may need to clean up and put out of sight works not intended for sale.

Space at a school, shopping-centre, church-hall, community venue.

Then away you go just like in your own gallery.

But keep in mind the space needed will not be great.

The toughest part is actually deciding what to do FIRST.

I had this problem once - I didn't know how to start a painting.

What I found out, and I suppose others have too, it didn't actually matter!

Just as long as it was something.

People, me before that, waste time working out the best thing to do.

Instead of starting and then turning that into the best thing they could.

That way procrastination also becomes a thing of the past!

These day's people are told to set goals to decide what to do.

This doesn't work if goal-setting is the activity as you still have to start.

It is better to do something even without goals than time deciding goals.

Particularly if you do not actually do anything.

But that's success secret #1: Get started.

It's really no secret – just something that has to be done!

The biggest thing plaguing people struggling is an inability to get started.

People are stuck on trying to figure out the details of their career.

Research, prepare, and make sure everything is "perfect" before they start!

It's unnecessary for that's really a way of putting it off for another day.
Usually that really means someone is scared!
Scared it's not going to work.
Scared you're going to look stupid.
Scared you might lose some money.
Scared you'll be judged.

So what if all that was GUARANTEED to happen?
Your friends will almost certainly judge you and talk behind your back.
They'll say what a fool you are for trying to make money as an artist.
At least one of them will believe you've fallen for a get-rich-quick scheme.
That's just the way it is.
So when is a good time to go full-time?

You've gone to art classes and workshops.
You've learnt lessons and your work is now something you are proud of.
You start to fantasize about a career as a full-time artist.
Maybe you always painted well and this is something you just want to do?
It doesn't matter!
The question is when is it a good time to go full time?

What are the criteria for making this decision?
The standard of your work is the most common one.
You are at the point where you think your work is good enough to sell.
But already you have made a mistake.
People do **NOT** buy on the basis of Is it good enough?

They buy what they like.
That may or may not be a 'good' work.
It all depends on what good is and who decides that.
To buy only the purchaser needs to think a work is good.

Some years ago a visitor to my studio saw a painting he really liked.
He asked how much was it?
I named a figure and a deal was made.
Although I had to sign the work first.
What he actually bought was my palette (which he still had to frame).

So you can sell anything if people want to buy it!
It's **NOT** what you or anyone else thinks that matters- only the buyer counts!
So back to when is the right time to become full time artist?
It's when you think it is, for that's when you are ready.
But that's not always the easiest way to be successful.
It may even be the fastest way to be unsuccessful!

A successful professional career is based on understanding basics.
They are **NOT** always what most artists believe!
It is widely assumed a professional career starts with an exhibition.
That **IS** when most people are aware of a professional career starting.
It is a 'coming out' a bit like making your debut at a ball.

But most exhibitions are abject failures.
But because of its public nature the failure is what is remembered.
You are behind the 8 ball already.
So surely that is **NOT** the way to **START** a **SUCCESSFUL** career!

Your first public exhibition has to be successful.
Then that is what is remembered but you must learn how to do that first!
So how do you learn how to sell **ALL** your artworks?
That means all of them at an exhibition!
Obviously you must start selling somewhere.
But like the artists of old you have to serve your apprenticeship.
This is not just learning how to paint.

You need to learn the business of being a professional.
Do you know how to sell?
What is the role of the frame in marketing your work?
How do you find potential clients (prospects)?

You can paint well but how many do you do in a given period of time.
As in any other business your productivity will influence your earnings.
Do you understand how to price your work?
Both now at the beginning and down the track too?
Can you manage your time effectively?
This will be hardest at the beginning.

If you can answer these questions think about a full-time career.
But also consider your outside responsibilities - family etc.?
If you do have them, you need to be more cautious than if by yourself.

Do you have finance?
No business – even that of an artist - can run without finance.
Money is the fuel that keeps business going.
You won't get it from sales at the start.

The ideal scenario:
Make the leap if you have a way of acquiring clients at break even or profit.
If you have an optimum selling system in place, then you have a business.

Do you have the professional basics in place?
If not what is missing and how well will you catch up?
Remember your job is to make a living!

Create and keep clients who buy your work or attend art classes.
You probably thought your main job was to paint or teach didn't you?
Yes, you do that, but as a professional artist it is so you can make a living.

Whatever you do you can only make a living with clients.
Clients are people who pay money for what you sell - it's really that simple.
It might be simple but that isn't the same as saying it's easy it's not!
The business climate is more competitive than ever.
The cost of acquiring a client is rising all the time.

You can easily spend a lot of money with little to show for it.
But it's not just money you'll spend; time also goes in large doses.
Fortunately maintaining clients you have, has time and money economies.
There is potential for increased sales as well - so it does get easier.

Enter everyone you know to start your contact list.
Do not worry about whether they buy your paintings at this stage either.
After all everyone has to start as someone who hasn't bought (yet)!
Don't worry about where they live just enter them, even incomplete details.
You may have an extensive list already.
Include the addresses of your friends and relatives.
That's if you want them to know about your exhibitions and other activities.
Enter everybody you do business with.
You'll need their addresses, email addresses and phone numbers.
Picture framer, galleries, or art shows organizers, publishers and others.
They have names and addresses of people interested in your work.

List galleries or art show organizers you haven't dealt with yet
But want to in the future.
It is important that you choose where you allow your work to be sold.
Then you take control of your career rather than drift.
Names, address, email address and phone number now before needed.

Don't forget electrician, solicitor, accountant, hairdresser, butcher.

Include all the people who depend on you for some of their income.
Your mechanic, car dealer, insurance representative, and many others.

Do not worry at all about whether they're likely to buy art or not!
This'll be quite a lot of people too - more than you think when you first start.
Don't worry about all the details are there or correct, enter what you can.
You support these people you can reasonably expect support from them.

Write down everybody you hope to do business with.
Go through old magazines, pieces of paper, or letters.
Obviously clients you'd like will be listed.
Anyone you know of who collects, or buys, artworks should be included.
Even include those who might possibly buy artworks.
Many are in the Yellow Pages headed 'Medical Practitioner' or 'Solicitor'.
Check back to the White Pages to find home address (not all will be there).

Write down other potential contacts for the future.
They are important group of people, including spouses and gatekeepers.
Gatekeepers are secretaries, or receptionists for important people.
They actually determine if you get to see or talk to the person concerned.
Their co-operation opens doors that would otherwise be hard to penetrate.

If you think you are starting to have a list that is too big, think again.
Collecting contact information is a standard part of professional activity.
Develop a routine although this may take quite a while to start with.
From art magazines list names and addresses who might be useful.

What about incomplete addresses?
Do detective work to find out the remaining information when it's needed.

Once you have started your contact list add to it all the time.

When you read a newspaper add to your list details of people you find.
Particularly those who might be useful one day.

This may take quite a while to start with.
As time goes by it does get easier, for many of the names are repeated.
You can automatically check if a person is on your list already or not.
Read your local paper every day, even if you live in a major city.
Note anyone who should be added to your list you may know them or not.
Obviously you'll have to do some detective work to find addresses.

Regularly update your list.
Those local papers will let you know when someone leaves your area.
Or they just help you add missing pieces to your jigsaw puzzle.

The best way to update is by phone.
Just ring and say you're updating your contact list.
Would it be OK to check on some information?
Most people do not mind as you are not asking them to buy anything.

The most important piece of information is the e-mail address.
They change regularly, that's why you need traditional contact
information.

A reason for calling is ask people do they mind being on your list?
This is a legal requirement so you have to do it.
Seek permission over the phone and get missing pieces at the same time.

Eventually you WILL cull your list.
That's when you know the right people from the rest.
But that takes time and you need everyone to start with.
What will you do when you know the right people from the rest?
Start converting prospects into long term repeat clients.

Cindy Johnson – Texas, USA wrote:
I'm keeping an ideas book.

I have found that my ideas book sets out things I want to paint.
Like subjects to paint, themes I'd like to explore, goals, timelines, etc.
It jogs me in a different way than my sketchbooks and keep me on track.

A yearly planner helps and I realize my goals are becoming clearer.
What I want most is to be on my feet and ready to **TAKE OFF**.
That's six and eight years from now when my son graduates high school.
He's ten.
I'd like to build up to that point when I have more and more time for my art.

Have a preliminary interview in another (specially set up) area.
This is where getting to know the prospect begins.
View each as the beginning of a long-term relationship with a collector.
Avoid making judgements about wealth of prospect based on appearance.
Just respond to answers to questions.

Ask what do you want the work for?
Where is it likely to hang?
Comfortable chair / lounge.
Special tea / coffee + signature RFS chocolates (indulgences).
Gather necessary information as per script.
Find out people's birthdays and acknowledge them, not a sales tactic.
Remember name, preferences not just for art but also tea / coffee.

Be polite at all times.
You must make prospect feel special and that you are there to help them.
Take time to understand what they are looking for or help them discover it.

CRM software can help build relationships.
A virtual book on preferences, important dates, personal information.
Track preferences and match with art database and link with client website.
Contact about new works arrived.

Contacts on birthday.

From the preliminary interview area a prospect can gain:
Identity from purchase – art collector – great decore – etc.
In the preliminary interview area you must:
Remember the prospect (appointment, preview interview, notes after visit).
Use prospect knowledge to suggest possible purchase option.
Develop links with a decorator to help prospect use the artwork as a focus.
You could endorse the decorator for added income (from decorator).

Then move into the Viewing Area.
Temperature control so warm in winter and cool in summer.
Should be easy access and close parking for at least two cars.

No advertising or promotion anywhere (not even for yourself).
Subtle use of lighting – highlight works, chocolates, special tea / coffee.
Use soft unobtrusive background music – this is **NOT** the focus.
Must be vaguely aware of the sound but that's it.
Probably classical music but should be appropriate to artwork.

Use scent, but subtle faint pleasant (spray Viewing Area before use).
Possibly incense.
Once the right smell has been discovered stick to it and don't vary.
Becomes a signature smell.

All details must harmonize.
You or anyone working for you dress so you blend with the atmosphere.
The focus is the client first and the work(s) second.
No 'hard sell'.
Ask questions.
Occasionally offer advice.
Design a set that works and then keep it.

There should be small changes for a prospect to notice (kind of chocolates).

Consider a Browsing Gallery.
Walls concertina like with one work per wall, so each is viewed individually.
Samples of the range of works are available.

Just sufficient to show range.
Say landscape, portrait, building, other subjects, in each medium used.
Generally they are small – samples.
Works on walls of Browsing Gallery on one side of gallery.
Seating on the other side.
Use subdued colour (like plum, magenta, dark bottle green, rich chocolate).
Use same images as in Viewing Area and Gallery, on website.
Smell fresh coffee, bread baking, lavender, fresh flowers.
Even old leather from furniture, old timber.
Generally they do not change.
Over time one may change and at a later date another.
This is how prospect decides what kind of work they like best.

Prospects make appointment to visit Browsing Gallery with friends.
Still get the coffee, chocolates, etc.
Can sit whilst in Browsing Gallery so can chat to friends, spouse etc.
There could be others in this gallery at the same time but not happen often.

Make buying your artwork a total experience.
The Viewing Area is for deciding which work to buy.
Here is where the prospect discovers something very special.
Keep the viewing area small.
Make being there a beautiful experience.
Sit to one side and slightly behind prospect so they focus on the work.
Not you.

Disappear to get the work to show.
Make it special so wear white gloves to protect the work.
Hang it on easel or wall very carefully – make it special.
Adjust the lighting – make it special.
Treat the work as if it is special.
Is it special to you because you want to sell it.
Make it seem as if you'd rather keep it.
No other area is available – they are a mystery.

Have special wrapping which is just yours.
A prospect must gain pleasure not just from the work but the act of buying.
Buying artworks, especially yours, should never be routine.
Maybe you associate with a certain colour?
Like Tiffany but your colour.
Once you decide do not vary after that.
You might have special packs just right for your standard sized works.
Say little but ask occasional questions when needed.
Possibly give something when the prospect leaves (brochure, whatever).
Gallery and Preview area must be clean and fresh.
Don't forget indoor plants.
Everything must fit together and provide a consistent brand image.
No clutter (unnecessary objects).

Make your website an extension of the Viewing area.
Use with referral website but not to start with.

Here are a few more thoughts:

Visualize success.
Success is getting to another level.
So imagine what that will actually feel like when you experience it.
Then you'll be more determined to make it a reality.
If you can think it, then you can achieve it!

Praise people around you.

By helping others build their self-confidence, they might in turn boost yours.

Just as importantly you'll appreciate ways confidence can be built.

Develop a sense of self-belief.

Make decisions based on the belief that you can do what you set out to do.

Don't give failure a chance.

Become more competent.

Set goals to improve your ability, skills and knowledge.

Do this regularly and consistently.

Champion sports people practice regularly!

Usually this is more than those who are not champions!

Believe in yourself.

This is the first step on the path to success, so you must at least do this.

Build from that beginning and make a series of small additional steps.

Reflect back from time to time to appreciate the progress you have made.

Grow through experience.

View mistakes as problems, challenges, and opportunities for experience.

You will grow every time you rise to a challenge and learn something.

Sometimes this is what not to do, at other times it will be worth repeating.

Savour your successes which at first they might be small.

That's how everyone starts.

Keep track of them, for that helps you realize later successes are better.

Turn negative situations into positive ones.

Increase your opportunities.

By expanding your network of people, new relationships open the door.

With new opportunities comes increasing confidence.

Surround yourself with success.

Mix with people who are successful and you'll learn to behave as they do. You'll build your confidence and be inspired by their attitudes.

Remember too, success is a journey not a destination.
You do not attain success but become successful.
Remember your BONUS!

Handmade chocolates will add a great touch to your next function.

Give your exhibition openings, print signings, or just visits to your studio a special flavour which will make a client or prospect remember their visit and want to return.

WHERE NEXT:

These are books that can help you build an art career:

You might need one or more of them:

http://www.amazon.com/dp/B087S87HLD
Productivity
http://www.amazon.com/dp/B087S85HS8
Price Right
http://www.amazon.com/dp/B087SCD1NY
Planning
http://www.amazon.com/dp/B087SCJYX3
Career Basics
http://www.amazon.com/dp/B087SM58GJ
Finding Buyers
http://www.amazon.com/dp/B087SFZ6RD
First Website
http://www.amazon.com/dp/B087SHDKPN
Successful Selling
http://www.amazon.com/dp/B087SGS6MB
Framing
http://www.amazon.com/dp/B087SHDKPN
Christmas
http://www.amazon.com/dp/B087SFTD61
Take the Plunge

NOT NOW:
There are other books that might interest you:

What about your own memories?
YOU could publish them – like I did!
To find out how - download this book.
http://www.amazon.com/dp/B087DWKPTP

There is a simple way to start developing creativity.
If you are a parent, teacher or someone who meets a group regularly?
To find out how - download this book:
http://www.amazon.com/dp/B088T1KFQZ

How do most people start to become an artist!
To find out how - download this book:
http://www.amazon.com/dp/B088Y1DPL6

There are more of my memories.
Find out what they are - download this book.
http://www.amazon.com/dp/B088Y4RPL9

SEND TO:

Know anyone interested in chocolate recipes?
If so they can download this book.
http://www.amazon.com/dp/B0882HK9Q9

Starting an art career is NOW is harder than it ever was.
To help someone start – they download this book.
http://www.amazon.com/dp/B088T7VJ76

A P P E N D I X :

CAREER SUMMARY:

Summary of creative enterprises commenced:
Founder Riverina Galleries, Wagga Wagga 1979 - 1997.
Founder of Riverina Framing (from 1980-90).
Developed ArtPak a correspondence course for artists (1995)
Published 'Art Professional' newsletters for artists.
Author "SPACE Art Education" for primary schools in NSW (1970 - 1982).

Summary of creative enterprises commenced with others:
Art consultant with NSW Department of Ed. from 1970-77 (Sydney).
Founder NSW Art Education Association (1970)
Art consultant with NSW Department of Ed. from 1980-81 (Riverina).
Consultant curator Charles Sturt University (1985-94).
Partner in Business Thinking Systems, Wagga Wagga (1999-2004).

Summary of related activity:
Graduate Bathurst Teachers College (1955).
Graduate National Art School (1970) distinctions in ALL final year subjects
Graduate Macquarie University (1979)
Taught general studies, art, art education, art philosophy.
In pre-school, infants, primary, secondary, university and adult education.
2 works hung in Wynne Prize (1969) (major Australian landscape award).
Won various art awards and had 22 one-man exhibitions.
Judged art shows in various parts of Australia.
Writes in 'Australian Artist' magazine each month, since 1995.
Writes in 'International Artist' magazine each two months, since 2002.
Wrote 'Coaching Creative Hockey' published by NSW Sport & Rec. (1974)
Coached Parkes Magpies, Parkes, Sydney University, University of NSW.
Selector Parkes, Sydney, NSW hockey.
Deputy President NSWHA.

Founder MG Car Club of Wagga Wagga.
Founder Gathering of the Faithful MG Car Club of Wagga Wagga.

www.ingramcontent.com/pod-product-compliance
Lightning Source LLC
Chambersburg PA
CBHW031250250726
48655CB00005B/2159